IMAGES
of America

LIGHTHOUSES OF
NEW HAMPSHIRE

This postcard from the early 1900s shows Portsmouth Harbor Lighthouse before it got its white exterior paint job in 1902, standing next to the 1860s-era wall of Fort Constitution. There has been a fort on this part of New Castle—known historically as Great Island—since the early 1630s. The present lighthouse is the third to be built at Fort Point, and its green light still welcomes mariners to Portsmouth Harbor as an active aid to navigation. (Author's collection.)

ON THE COVER: Portsmouth Harbor Lighthouse and the wall of Fort Constitution are pictured around 1870. Seen to the left of center in the background is Wood Island, which at that time was home to a quarantine hospital. A lifesaving station was built on the island in 1873. Seen in the center background is Whaleback Lighthouse, just across the border in Maine. Barely visible in the distance are the Isles of Shoals, about six miles away. (Courtesy of Ed Stevenson.)

IMAGES
of America

LIGHTHOUSES OF
NEW HAMPSHIRE

Jeremy D'Entremont

ARCADIA
PUBLISHING

Published by Arcadia Publishing
Charleston, South Carolina

Printed in the United States of America

Library of Congress Control Number: 2023951537

For all general information, please contact Arcadia Publishing:
Telephone 843-853-2070
Fax 843-853-0044
E-mail sales@arcadiapublishing.com

Visit us on the Internet at www.arcadiapublishing.com

In memory of Connie Small—author, artist, and guiding light.

CONTENTS

ACKNOWLEDGMENTS

Many of the images included in this book are from my own collection, garnered over almost 40 years of lighthouse research. But this book would not be possible without the kind assistance of many people and organizations, including (but not limited to) the New Castle Historical Society, the Portsmouth Athenaeum, the Portsmouth Historical Society, the US Coast Guard, the Lake Sunapee Protective Association, the Sunapee Historical Society, the Portsmouth Public Library, the Lighthouse Kids, the American Lighthouse Foundation, Bob Trapani Jr., the US Lighthouse Society, Jim Claflin, Kraig Anderson, Carol White, and Jeff Gales. Lighthouse Kids founder Sue Reynolds, whose passion for the Isles of Shoals is unmatchable, has always been generous with her time and historical collection. I want to acknowledge the late Jane Porter, the longtime keeper of the Portsmouth Athenaeum and author of the book *Friendly Edifices: Piscataqua Lighthouses and Other Aids to Navigation*. Jane generously shared her invaluable research materials with me, and her book remains the definitive source on the lighthouses of our area. Thanks also to J. Dennis Robinson, who has been the most thoughtful and thorough historian of the New Hampshire Seacoast region. Dennis's books and articles are a treasure for anyone looking into the history of the area. I also need to acknowledge the woman who served as a guiding light to so many in this region, the late Connie Small. It was a rare privilege to know Connie, who was the wife of the last keeper of Portsmouth Harbor Lighthouse and author of the classic book *The Lighthouse Keeper's Wife*. A big tip of my baseball cap also to several ex-Coast Guardsmen and Isles of Shoals light keepers with whom I have corresponded. This includes Kevin Madison, Rick Bennett, Glenn Young, Harold Roberts, Rick Loster, and Ed Latta. I apologize to anyone I may have omitted. Please know that all of you have my sincere gratitude.

INTRODUCTION

New Hampshire has the shortest seacoast (about 18 miles) of any state in the United States that has a seacoast. But the region has played a major role in the country's history, from the early settlement in Rye in the 1620s to the prominence of the Isles of Shoals as one of the world's major fishing ports to the important role of Portsmouth as the colonial capital and a center of trade. Although there are only two lighthouses on the seacoast—one on the mainland (Portsmouth Harbor Light) and one offshore (White Island)—each of them has a long and varied history.

The human history of these lighthouses includes Joshua Card, keeper for 35 years at Portsmouth Harbor. He was 86 at the time of his retirement, the oldest lighthouse keeper in the country. Later, Elson Small served as Portsmouth Harbor Lighthouse's last keeper in the 1940s, and his wife, Connie, later achieved wide acclaim as the author of *The Lighthouse Keeper's Wife*. At White Island, Celia Thaxter, the daughter of keeper Thomas Laighton, became one of the most beloved poets and authors in 19th-century America. In more recent times, local teacher Sue Reynolds and the intrepid Lighthouse Kids have been an inspiration as they worked to save endangered White Island Lighthouse.

The three wooden lighthouses on inland Lake Sunapee were not built by the federal government and might not be considered by some to be "real" lighthouses, but they have served navigation on the lake for well over a century. Lake Sunapee, with its stunning natural beauty, has been a busy resort dating back to the halcyon days of grand hotels and steamship travel in the late 1800s. To locals, the lighthouses on the lake are just as beloved as any coastal beacon.

Lighthouses—or at least aids to navigation that can be considered to be primitive lighthouses—date back to ancient times. The Pharos of Alexandria, built in the Nile Delta in the 3rd century BC, is often cited as the first significant lighthouse in the world. The remains of three ancient Roman lighthouses still stand in England, Turkey, and Libya. Other early lighthouses stand at Hook Head in Ireland; in Galicia, Spain (the Tower of Hercules); and at Genoa, Italy.

By the time Boston Light came along as the first lighthouses in the North American British colonies, there were still only a small number of lighthouses in the world. By this time, the early use of coal fires on top of towers had advanced to spermaceti candles and subsequently to fish oil and whale oil lamps. More lighthouses soon followed at places like the important whaling port of Nantucket and near centers of trade like Newport, Rhode Island, and New London, Connecticut. Before 1771, all the lighthouses in the British colonies in North America were south of Boston.

Native Americans had inhabited the seacoast region for thousands of years before Europeans arrived in the early 1600s. The area near the mouth of the Piscataqua River, actually a tidal estuary with a swift current, provided a natural harbor and led to the commercial development of Portsmouth. Unlike the contemporary colony at Plymouth, which began in the name of religious freedom, Portsmouth was founded for purely capitalistic reasons.

The Laconia Company in England had backed an earlier settlement at Dover, New Hampshire, but that one failed after a few years. In 1630, another group financed by the Laconia Company set up a permanent settlement in the waterfront area of Portsmouth that is now the Strawbery Banke Museum and Prescott Park.

The group believed there was money to be made in the mining of precious metals in the area, along with fishing and trade. The mining hopes led to nothing, but the settlement prospered anyway. At the time of its incorporation as a town in 1653, Portsmouth was named in honor of John Mason, the colony's founder. He had been the captain of the port of Portsmouth, England.

The nearby forests in New Hampshire and Maine provided abundant lumber, and the Portsmouth area became a leader in shipbuilding in the 1600s. The early vessels built in Portsmouth or just on the other side of the Piscataqua in Kittery, Maine, include the HMS *Falkland*, the first British warship built in the American colonies, and the *Raleigh*, the first vessel to carry the American flag in battle (1776). The *Ranger*, launched in 1777, was captained by John Paul Jones during his attack on British interests during the American Revolution. Just over a decade later in 1800, the Portsmouth Naval Shipyard (technically on the Kittery side of the river) began operation. It is now the oldest continuously operating shipyard of the US Navy.

The fishing industry in the region also developed in the 17th century. There was a great demand for cod in Europe, and fishermen were crossing the Atlantic to fish around the Isles of Shoals—the nine-island archipelago a few miles off the New Hampshire coast—by the early 1600s. If not for fishing, the islands might never have been inhabited. Robert Thayer Sterling, in his 1935 book *Maine Lighthouses and the Men Who Keep Them*, aptly described the Isles of Shoals as "a low lying group apparently composed of masses of tumbled granite bleached white by the unceasing beating of the storm king and the glare of the blazing sun."

Fishermen began settling on the islands, and in 1675, there were about 275 people living in the Isles of Shoals. The American Revolution and the War of 1812 brought about the end of the year-round fishing settlement, but the late 1800s saw the development of the island group as a center of tourism.

By the early 1800s, although fishing had declined, there was still a small population on the islands. It was felt that a lighthouse on White Island, at the southernmost of the Isles of Shoals, would help guide shipping traffic toward Portsmouth and would be an aid to help coastal shipping avoid the York Ledges to the north. Congress appropriated $5,000 for the lighthouse in 1820, and it was quickly built.

The lighthouses at Portsmouth Harbor and the Isles of Shoals remain active aids to navigation, with the automatic lights turning on each night with the help of daylight sensors. But the importance of these lighthouses as historic monuments today outweighs their navigational value. They stand as icons pointing to centuries of New Hampshire seacoast maritime history, and they stand as testaments to their builders and resident keepers. And besides, who doesn't love a lighthouse?

One

PORTSMOUTH HARBOR
LIGHTHOUSE

Well protected and seldom frozen over, the harbor of Portsmouth, New Hampshire, near the mouth of the Piscataqua River, was one of the busiest ports of colonial America. It remains the only deepwater port on New Hampshire's short 18-mile seacoast. The town of New Castle, once known as Great Island, is linked by bridges to Portsmouth and Rye. New Castle was a thriving fishing village for many years, and it was the first capital of the province of New Hampshire. Jutting out from the northeast corner of the town—about a mile from the entrance to the Piscataqua River—is the finger of land known as Fort Point, named for the fortifications that have been located there for nearly four centuries. There has been a lighthouse at Fort Point since before the American Revolution, and today's iconic tower is the third lighthouse structure in the history of the site. Locals know it as Fort Point Light, but it is generally referred to in official documents as Portsmouth Harbor Lighthouse. It is a familiar icon of the region and was used in the logo of the Portsmouth Historical Society's celebration of the 400th anniversary of European settlement in the region.

The Piscataqua River, which separates the New Hampshire coast from the Maine coast, takes its name from an Abenaki word that is often translated as "many rivers flowing into one." The reason for the name is apparent on this map, which is rotated nearly 90 degrees clockwise so that east is at the bottom. The Cochecho, Bellamy, Lamprey, Exeter, and Oyster Rivers all converge into the 12-mile-long Piscataqua, which features some of the strongest tides of any navigable river in the country. The area was explored by Europeans as early as 1603, and English outposts were established by 1623. The settlement that became the city of Portsmouth was known as Strawbery Banke, named for the wild berries that grew in abundance. This map was created in the late 1800s, based on an original from around 1670. (Maine State Archives.)

Portsmouth Harbor grew to prominence just inside the mouth of the Piscataqua. The harbor was strategically placed between industries upstream and trade interests along the coast and abroad. Shipbuilding on the Piscataqua was well established by the mid-1600s, and the harbor continued to flourish in the 1700s. By 1774, nearly 200 ships called Portsmouth their home port. This painting shows Portsmouth around 1774. (Currier Museum of Art.)

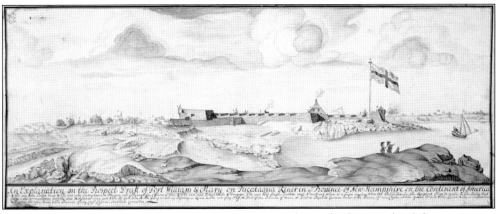

New Castle, once known as Great Island, is about a mile inside the mouth of the Piscataqua. The first fort on Great Island dates to the early days of the Strawbery Banke settlement in 1631. Commonly known as "The Castle," the fort was enlarged and renamed Fort William and Mary in 1692. (Norman B. Leventhal Map Center at the Boston Public Library.)

In 1765, a group of concerned citizens wrote to the New Hampshire legislature "that the Necessity of a Light house at some Suitable place near the Mouth of Piscataqua harbor is . . . Obvious to every One acquainted with the Situation." Capt. Titus Salter, one of Portsmouth's leading merchants, was one of the petitioners. Salter would later become a keeper of the lighthouse. (Author's collection.)

A schooner carrying molasses was wrecked off the entrance to the harbor in 1768, adding fuel to the call for a lighthouse. Royal governor John Wentworth made his case: "I trust the Honble Assembly will enable me to establish this Light, and that we shall participate with ev'ry Contributor in the Blessings of our fellow Creatures whose Lives may thus be rescued from Death." (New York Public Library Digital Collections.)

An act to establish a light was passed by the legislature in April 1771. The light was paid for by a duty on all shipping entering the harbor. A simple lantern on a flagstaff was considered, but that idea was deemed "impracticable," and a lighthouse was quickly built. As indicated in this notice to local mariners, the lighthouse went into service on June 8, 1771. (Author's collection.)

1 7. 5 1:
NEW-HAMPSHIRE.
NOTICE is HEREBY Given,
to all Mariners, That on the Night of the 8th Day of June next, will be illuminated a
Light-House,
for the Benefit and Direction of Vessels, bound into this Harbour : The Edifice is now erecting, upon the Eastermost part of Fort-Point (so called) at the entrance of Piscataqua Harbour, and will be lighted up every Night.

The Printers of News-Papers, it is hoped will publish this Advertisement in their several Papers, for the Information and Benefit of Maritime Persons, within the Spheres of their respective Circulations.

Portsmouth, April 17, 1771.

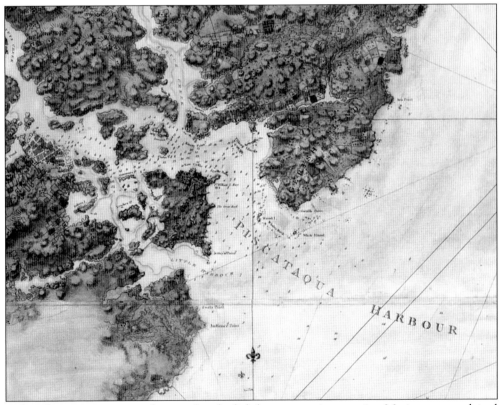

Sailing directions were issued soon after the lighthouse went into service. Mariners were advised that on entering the Piscataqua River, they should "keep in twelve Fathom of Water until the Light bears North, North one half West, Distance about three Miles, and then bear away for the Light House . . . giving the Light a proper Birth [sic]. The deep center of the Piscataqua remains the primary channel into the harbor today. (Author's collection.)

Later in 1771, Governor Wentworth extolled the lighthouse: "Already it hath been the acknowledged means of preserving two vessels and their men. In all probability it will afford the same Benefit to many others." Portsmouth native Daniel Brewster, the 35-year-old builder of the tower, was paid a sum of 372 pounds, 11 shillings, and a single penny in January 1772. His pay was delayed until well after the lighthouse was built because the funds originally appropriated for the project had been put to other uses. The shingled wooden tower was topped by an iron lantern, with the light produced by three oil lamps made of copper. It was the 10th of 11 light stations established in the colonies before the American Revolution, and the first lighthouse in the American colonies north of Boston. The French naval artist Pierre Ozanne (1737–1813) created this view of Portsmouth Harbor and the original lighthouse. (Author's collection.)

This is a portion of a 1779 drawing titled *View of Piscataqua Lighthouse from Kitterie point.* Although it appears to be hundreds of feet tall compared to the fort buildings, the 1771 tower stood only about 50 feet tall. It is possible that the artist was emphasizing the importance of the lighthouse by exaggerating its size. (Author's collection.)

Whereas the General-Assembly of the Province of New-Hampshire has granted Twenty-four Pounds Proclamation Money, to pay an able Man for attending the LIGHT-HOUSE within said Province, for one Year— Whosoever is willing to undertake the same, may, by applying immediately at the Secretary's-Office, or to Capt. John Cockran's at Castle William & Mary, enter upon the Business.
Portsmouth, June 1, 1774.

In the years leading to the American Revolution, the commander of Fort William and Mary was also in charge of the lighthouse. The commander when the lighthouse was built was Capt. John Cochran, who was born in Ireland. This advertisement was published in the *New Hampshire Gazette* on June 1, 1774, as an attempt to find someone to help with the maintenance of the lighthouse.

In December 1774, hundreds of local men raided Fort William and Mary and successfully made off with ammunition and cannons, an action that is considered by many to be the first overt skirmish of the American Revolution. After surrendering to the invaders, Captain Cochran was released and remained with the British Army during the American Revolution. Howard Pyle depicted the surrender of Fort William and Mary in this illustration. (Author's collection.)

The light was extinguished during the American Revolution, although the tower was utilized as a lookout post. The lighthouse was repaired and put back into service in 1784. The lighting apparatus at that time was an open copper pan with seven wicks, known as a "spider lamp." The fuel used was fish oil. This document is a bill for repairs carried out in 1784. (Author's collection.)

A Pay Roll for attending the light at Fort Point from July 22 up to & including 20th Octr.

Name	Time of Engagemt	wages p month	Time of Servis	wages Due	Total Sum		
Elias Tarlton	July .. 22	£ 2	2 mos 28 days	£5.17.4		Elias Tarlton	
					£5.17.4		

A True Roll
Pr Nathan Bell Lt Comdt

Factor 17 Decr 1784 ——
Then received an Order on the Treasr for the above
Sum of five pounds seventeen shillings & fourpence
In behalf of Elias Tarlton
Geo Gains

For some years in the 1780s, the day-to-day care of the lighthouse was delegated to Elias Tarlton, a soldier at the fort who was born in New Castle around 1720. There was no housing for Tarlton inside the fort, so he walked a few hundred yards from his home in New Castle. Records show that he was paid 5 pounds, 17 shillings, and 4 pence for the care of the lighthouse from July 22 to October 20, 1784, as seen in this document. (Author's collection.)

The lighthouse and fort were ceded to the federal government in February 1791. A few months later, a fire broke out in the lantern during a trial using whale oil. Joseph Whipple, the local lighthouse superintendent, reported that whale oil burned much brighter than the fish oil then in use. Lamps better suited to whale oil were installed by 1793. (The Corcoran Collection, National Gallery.)

Tench Coxe, pictured here, was appointed commissioner of revenue by President Washington in 1792. Five years later, Coxe called keeper David Duncan to task in a letter to Joseph Whipple. Duncan had been using more oil than the keepers at the other lighthouses then in service. "The misuse of the public stores is always to be guarded against," wrote Coxe. In spite of this, Duncan remained keeper for 27 years. (Author's collection.)

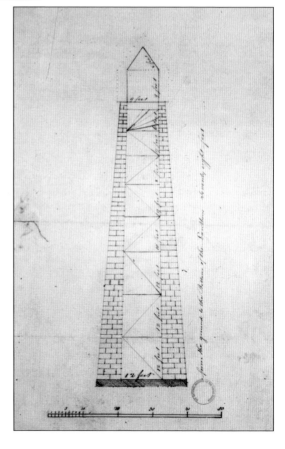

Local merchants petitioned for a repositioning of the lighthouse in 1793. Tench Coxe concurred that the light was not "in the best possible place." Joseph Whipple suggested Pollock Rock, close to 100 yards to the southeast—a location that would be more advantageous to shipping than the 1771 site. A bill was passed in 1802 for a new tower on Pollock Rock. A wooden structure was designed, 78 feet tall to the base of the lantern. (National Archives.)

The octagonal tower was built in 1804 of pine on a stone foundation. The builder was Benjamin Clark Gilman, a prominent builder and clockmaker from nearby Exeter, New Hampshire. Local author John Albee described the lighthouse in his 1884 book *New Castle: Historic and Picturesque*: "It straddled the rocks like a modern Colossus." (Author's collection.)

Seen here is another view of the 1804 lighthouse, as drawn sometime later in the 1800s. The fort had been rebuilt and enlarged around 1808 and renamed Fort Constitution. David Duncan, who had been keeper since 1793, remained in charge of the new lighthouse until 1820. When the new lighthouse was built, the old one was dismantled and the wood was sold. (Author's collection.)

Civil engineer I.W.P. Lewis visited the station for his 1843 report to Congress. He noted that Portsmouth was the only harbor "of any capacity" in the area and that it was "well known as amongst the best, though rather dangerous of access." Lewis called the lighthouse an "excellent piece of carpentry" that would "bear favorable comparison with its more modern neighbors." Lewis pointed out that the light had fallen to "the grade of a simple harbor beacon" with the establishment of Whaleback Light at the mouth of the Piscataqua in 1831. He offered the opinion that the number of lamps could be reduced from 13 to one, and the height of the tower "might be advantageously reduced to thirty feet." The tower was shortened to 55 feet by the end of 1851. (US Coast Guard Historian's Office.)

This is another view of the 1804 lighthouse after it had been shortened, around 1859. The lantern was fitted with a fourth-order Fresnel lens in 1854. Meanwhile, with the formation of the US Lighthouse Board in 1852, more highly qualified keepers were sought. New keepers had to be able to read and write, keep simple financial accounts, know how to row and sail a small boat, and have sufficient skill to maintain lighthouse equipment and perform minor repairs as needed. (Portsmouth Athenaeum.)

Work began in 1862 on a large "Third System" fort, which was to include a three-tiered granite wall constructed outside of the 1808 outer walls of Fort Constitution. Masonry forts were becoming obsolete as the Civil War progressed, and construction was halted by 1867. This view shows the lighthouse next to the granite wall then under construction. (New York Public Library.)

21

A new one-and-one-half-story keeper's house was built in 1872, on the foundation of the previous house, after an appropriation of $2,000. The 1872 keeper's house was built near the remains of the Walbach Tower, a War of 1812 gun emplacement. The house was about 1,000 feet to the west of the lighthouse. Notice the lighthouse keeper standing by the house. (National Archives.)

Walbach Tower, Built in 1812, Newcastle, N. H.

The Walbach Tower near the keeper's house has a fascinating history of its own. It was constructed during the War of 1812 as part of the effort to protect Portsmouth Harbor from attack. It is similar to many structures built across the British Empire that were known as Martello Towers, which typically had a single artillery piece mounted on top. It was named for John de Barth Walbach, the officer in charge of Fort Constitution. (Author's collection.)

A new 48-foot cast-iron lighthouse tower was erected in 1878 on the same foundation as the 1804 tower. The cast-iron segments were prepared in a Portland, Maine, foundry. It was noted in a newspaper account that when the heavy timbers of the 1804 tower were cut away to make room for the new one, the wood was "found as sound as when first put in." (Portsmouth Athenaeum.)

The 1878 tower was built under the supervision of Army Corps officer James Chatham Duane (1824–1897). Duane was chief engineer of the Army of the Potomac during the Civil War. After the war, he served as an engineer for the US Lighthouse Board. Under Duane's supervision, about a dozen cylindrical cast-iron lighthouse towers were built in the Northeast. (Friends of Portsmouth Harbor Lighthouses.)

About a mile from Portsmouth Harbor Lighthouse, at the mouth of the Piscataqua River, a lighthouse was built at Whaleback (or Whalesback) Ledge in 1830. The ledge is about 1,500 feet on the Maine side of the border with New Hampshire. Although it is the southernmost lighthouse in Maine, historically it was classified as a New Hampshire lighthouse because it marks the entrance to Portsmouth Harbor. The first lighthouse was poorly built. The stone tower was sheathed in wood to stop leaks, but during a storm in 1837, some of the small stones in the inner walls of the tower fell out onto the floors of the rooms and furniture moved about as the tower shook. The keepers lived in fear that the tower might not survive, but somehow the original lighthouse stood for more than 40 years and has been described as the first successful wave-swept lighthouse in the United States. The important new light on Whaleback Ledge led to the lowering of the height and visibility of Portsmouth Harbor Lighthouse. (National Archives.)

A new 70-foot-tall granite lighthouse was built on Whaleback Ledge in 1872, and it still stands today. In the summer of 1878, an unusual cast-iron tower was built next to the lighthouse to serve as a fog signal house. The tower was surmounted by a third-class fog trumpet that emitted an eight-second blast every 30 seconds. The fog signal tower was painted red for some years. In late June 1882, assistant keeper John Lewis fell from the tower as he was painting the apex of the pipe that held the foghorn. A tugboat transported him to shore, but he died from his injuries several days later at his home in Kittery. Although the lighthouse is officially in Maine waters, some of the best views are from the New Hampshire coast in Rye and New Castle. (US Coast Guard.)

The footbridge connecting the lighthouse to the shore has been rebuilt and reconfigured many times over the years. It was noted that it was 300 feet long at the time of repairs in 1832. It was 325 feet long when it was rebuilt in 1847. According to the US Lighthouse Board's annual report for 1863, it was rebuilt that year after it was removed to "facilitate operations on the fortifications." (Portsmouth Athenaeum.)

This view at low tide from the late 1800s shows the footbridge leading to a trail along the water's edge, next to the fence, which led eventually to the keeper's house. The fence seen here was later replaced by a sea wall, but in spite of the added protection, the area inside the wall has been badly flooded during storms multiple times in recent years. (Maine Lighthouse Museum.)

Each of the cast-iron cylinders that make up the tower is made of 12 individual cast-iron plates, fastened with nuts and bolts. The cast-iron lighthouse was still rare in New England when the Portsmouth tower was built. John Albee of New Castle, in his book *New Castle: Historic and Picturesque*, called it "hideous" and described it as "a corpulent length of stove pipe, set on end—and painted." Despite some early resistance to the style, the present tower is a handsome example of the durable, low-maintenance, brick-lined, cast-iron lighthouses developed by the US Lighthouse Board. It displays design features that were not present in pre-1870s lighthouse towers, including three arched windows with Italianate hood molds. The exterior of the lighthouse was painted brown until August 1902, when it was painted white. (James W. Claflin.)

This view from the late 1870s shows the new cast-iron lighthouse along with the partially completed granite wall of Fort Constitution. The footbridge that provided access to the lighthouse at this time ran parallel to the shore and was much longer than in later years. (Friends of Portsmouth Harbor Lighthouses.)

This photograph was likely taken in 1878, shortly after the construction of the cast-iron lighthouse but before a new cast-iron fog signal building was constructed alongside Whaleback Lighthouse. Whaleback can be seen in this photograph to the right of the sailboat in the distance. Also seen here is Wood Island, later the site of a lifesaving station. At this time a quarantine hospital was located on the island. (Friends of Portsmouth Harbor Lighthouses.)

This view from around 1870 shows Parrot rifles in Fort Constitution's embrasures. These guns remained in place until 1905. The Army deactivated the fort in 1948, along with the rest of the nearby forts defending Portsmouth Harbor. In 1973, Fort Constitution was placed in the National Register of Historic Places. The fort's gatehouse was rebuilt in 1974. (Ed Stevenson.)

A bronze, 1,048-pound fog bell was added to the station in early 1896. "During thick or foggy weather," it was announced, "the bell will be struck by machinery, a single blow every ten seconds." The bell was mounted on a small square shed with a flat roof, adjoining the base of the lighthouse tower. Striking machinery for the bell was inside the shed. (Portsmouth Athenaeum.)

This late-1800s image shows a cluster of buildings on the left that were related to the fort and lighthouse, most of which are now gone. The white building just to the left of center was recently sold by the Coast Guard to the Town of New Castle. This version of the footbridge to the lighthouse was much longer than the one that was built after the 1906 move of the keeper's house. (US Coast Guard.)

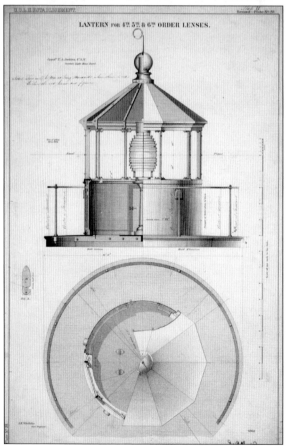

The fourth-order Fresnel lens that had been installed in 1854 was transferred to the cast-iron lantern atop the 1878 tower. A fixed white light was shown from the new lighthouse on the night after it was last shown from the old one. As lard oil was being phased out, this was the first lighthouse in the United States to have kerosene-burning apparatus as part of its original equipment. (National Archives.)

A 1935 inspection report indicates that the lens had been manufactured by L. Sautter and Company of Paris. The lens that is still in use in the lighthouse today, however, was manufactured by Henri-Lepaute of Paris. In October 1925, the keeper recorded that the lens was badly cracked in an accident, and it seems likely that a new lens was installed sometime after 1935. (Friends of Portsmouth Harbor Lighthouses.)

In 1879, the footbridge to the lighthouse—160 feet long at the time—was again rebuilt. It was rebuilt yet again a decade later, and the length was reported as 320 feet. This c. 1900 photograph is a view from the rocks outside the wall of Fort Constitution. The lighthouse was still painted brown, and the fog bell is clearly seen. (Friends of Portsmouth Harbor Lighthouses.)

This c. 1900 image shows tourists viewing the fort and lighthouse. Giving tours was part of the job for keepers. The instructions stated, "The light-keeper is expected to be polite to strangers, in showing the premises at such hours as do not interfere with the proper duties of his office. The light keeper must not, on any pretext, admit persons in a state of intoxication into the lighthouse." (Friends of Portsmouth Harbor Lighthouses.)

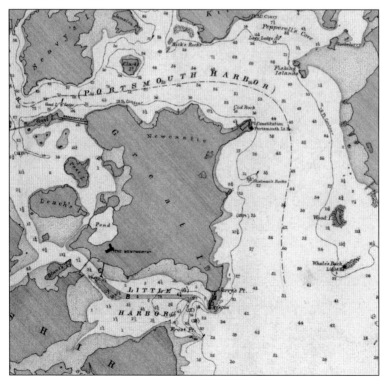

Seen near the lower left on this 1884 map is Little Harbor, between New Castle and Rye. On the north side of the entrance to Little Harbor is Jerry's Point, also known as Jaffrey Point. A small light at the end of a breakwater at this location, identified on the map as "beacon," was maintained for many years by the keeper at Portsmouth Harbor Lighthouse. (National Archives.)

The keeper who served the longest in the station's history was Joshua Kenney Card, who was born in New Castle in a home overhanging the Piscataqua River in 1822. His ancestors were said to be among the earliest English settlers in New Castle. His father was held prisoner during the War of 1812, and both of his grandfathers served in the American Revolution. An older brother was lost at sea at the age of 21. Card made his first voyage as a 12-year-old cabin boy on the fishing schooner *Hope*, on a four-month voyage with his father as first mate. He worked on fishing vessels until 1849, sailing as far as Cuba. When his father went to California for the Gold Rush in 1849, Card took a position at the Portsmouth Naval Shipyard. Later, for a number of years, he ran a stagecoach known as the New Castle Express between New Castle and Portsmouth. (New Castle Historical Society.)

In 1867, Joshua Card took the position of principal lighthouse keeper at Boon Island, seen here, several miles up the coast from Portsmouth off the coast of southern Maine. He later recalled a giant wave that swept across the island, leaving water two feet deep in the lighthouse tower. During his time at Boon Island, Card achieved the distinction of having the highest salary of any American lighthouse keeper, $860 per year. (National Archives.)

(FORM NO. 5.)

VOUCHER FOR KEEPER'S SALARY.

U. S. Light-House Establishment,

To *Joshua K. Card*, *Dr.*

1876. (*Appropriation for* *Light Keepers Salaries*)

DATE.		DOLLARS.	CTS.
For salary as (a) Keeper of the Light (b) *house* at *Portsmouth Harbor*, from the *1* day of *April* to the *30* day of *June*, 1876, inclusive, at $ *500.* per annum		*125*	

(c) I HEREBY CERTIFY that *I* have actually performed the services stated in the above account.

Joshua K. Card
Keeper.

RECEIVED, this *3* day of *July* . 1876, of *A. F. Horrard* Superintendent of Lights, &c., for the District of *Portsmouth*, the sum of *One hundred twenty five* ⁴/₁₀₀ Dollars, in full of the above account.

$ *125,* (SIGNED DUPLICATES.)

Joshua K. Card
Keeper.

WITNESS: *S. H. Marshall*

(a) State whether *principal* or *assistant* keeper.
(b) State whether *light-house* or *light-vessel*.
(c) If the voucher is for an *assistant* keeper's salary, the principal keeper must sign the certificate; if for a *principal* keeper, he will sign it himself.

With the harsh conditions at Boon Island, it was no wonder that Joshua Card took a substantial pay cut (from $860 to $500 per year) to take the keeper's position at Portsmouth Harbor. This is a pay voucher from the second quarter of 1876. Keepers at remote, offshore stations like Boon Island were paid more than the keepers at the relatively peaceful mainland stations like Portsmouth Harbor. (Friends of Portsmouth Harbor Lighthouses.)

Keeper Joshua Card and his wife, Dolly Ann (Beal), had six children, one of whom died in infancy. Dolly Card died in 1886. A 1908 article in the *Portsmouth Daily Chronicle* praised the 85-year-old keeper: "In thirty-five years his light has been in charge of a substitute but eleven nights altogether, and although he is eighty-five years old the lighthouse inspectors all agree that there is not a more efficient man in the service. Despite his age, Captain Card is hale and hearty, vigorous and alert. . . . The regular summer residents are all friends of the veteran light keeper. They call each year to pay their respect upon their arrival and to say good-by when leaving in the fall." The civilian US Lighthouse Service uniform at the time bore the letter "K," for keeper, on the lapels. It was reported that when visitors asked Card what the "K" stood for, he would tell them, "Why, captain, of course." (Portsmouth Athenaeum.)

Keeper Card retired in March 1909 at the age of 86 due to failing health. The *Portsmouth Herald* reported in August 1910 that the former keeper had "the respect of every man, woman, and child" in New Castle. Card died in June 1911 at the home of his daughter in Newburyport, Massachusetts. A letter published in the *Portsmouth Herald* sang Card's praises: "Punctual to the minute, he literally stayed at his post year after year without a break. At least during this extraordinarily long term he was absent, I am told, but once, and that only for a few days. Moreover, at the date when old age had admonished him that he should retire from active duty, Captain Card was, I believe, in point of continuous service, the oldest lighthouse keeper on the coast. He loved the town, and the townspeople loved him. His remains rest upon the bank of the beautiful river, the ebb and flow of whose tides for many a long year had entered into the daily routine of his useful and honorable life." (Strawbery Banke Museum.)

In September 2016, volunteers and staff of the American Lighthouse Foundation and Friends of Portsmouth Harbor Lighthouses gathered with friends and supporters for the dedication of a US Lighthouse Service marker at keeper Joshua Card's gravesite at the Riverside Cemetery in New Castle. Also taking part were descendants of Card. (American Lighthouse Foundation.)

This early-1900s advertisement for the Portsmouth Chamber of Commerce features superimposed high seas coming from the north at an unlikely angle. The city of Portsmouth has long been a tourist destination known for its restaurants and cultural scene. In 2009, *National Geographic's Traveler* ranked Portsmouth sixth in the country for historical places to visit. (Author's collection.)

The lighthouse tower was painted white in 1902, and it has remained that color since then. As seen in this photograph, shades (or curtains) inside the glass of the lantern room were always pulled down during the day. The shades were a precaution against the hazard of the prisms magnifying the sun's rays onto a burner holding combustible kerosene. It was also felt that direct exposure to the sun could, over time, cause a slight color change in the glass of the lens and that the heat could weaken the litharge (putty) that held the prisms together. The curtains were removed from their hangers at dusk, just before the keeper lit the lamp for the night. The old stone base from the 1804 tower is seen here, whitewashed by the keeper. (National Archives.)

An inspection in 1903 revealed that the kerosene for the light, along with kerosene for the small light at Jaffrey Point—a mile south of Portsmouth Harbor Light Station—was being stored in an old wooden building on the station. Funds were soon appropriated for two small brick oil houses, one at each location. Notice the low stone wall around the oil house in this view from 1947, an attempt to protect the foundation in high tides. (National Archives.)

The 1872 keeper's house was moved twice to make room for new military batteries. Since 1906, the dwelling has been within the granite Civil War–era walls of Fort Constitution atop a foundation of massive granite blocks. When the house was moved to the present site, a new footbridge, about 84 feet long, was constructed from the nearby 1860s-era outer granite wall on the south side of Fort Constitution to the lighthouse. (Friends of Portsmouth Harbor Lighthouses.)

Fort Point Light, New Castle, N. H.

Under the keeper's house was a basement that held a 2,000-gallon brick cistern, in which rainwater was collected for the use of the keeper and his family. In the 1910–1911 period, improvements made to the keeper's house included the installation of indoor plumbing and the welcome addition of a bathroom. (Friends of Portsmouth Harbor Lighthouses.)

Leander White, seen here with his wife, Elizabeth, began his lightkeeping career as an assistant at Maine's Boon Island Light in 1874. He served as principal keeper at three Maine light stations before taking charge at Portsmouth Harbor Lighthouse in 1909. A newspaper reported, "Capt. White is the fourth oldest keeper in point of service in this district, having served 37 years. He is one of the best men in this dept. of the government." He retired in 1915. (Chuck Petlick.)

Fort Point Light, New Castle, N. H.

Welcome to

New Castle

The Best Town in the Country

This c. 1913 postcard sang the praises of the town of New Castle, the smallest (.81 square miles of land and 1.5 square miles of water) and easternmost town in New Hampshire and the only one situated entirely on islands. New Castle, originally called Great Island by English settlers, takes its name from the early fort established there by 1632. New Castle was the provincial capital of New Hampshire for some years, and it was incorporated in 1693. Today, the picturesque town is best known as the location of the elegant Wentworth-by-the-Sea Hotel and the site of Fort Stark, the Harbor Defense Command Post in World War II. Of course, it is also famous as the location of Fort Constitution and Portsmouth Harbor Lighthouse. (Author's collection.)

CONFERENCE BUILDING

RUSSIA - JAPAN
PEACE CONFERENCE
AUGUST, 1905

THE GATEWAY TO THE HARBOR

Greetings from *The Finlaysons*

This postcard, calling the lighthouse the "gateway to the harbor," commemorated the signing of the Treaty of Portsmouth in September 1905. The treaty ended the Russo-Japanese War of 1904–1905. Formal negotiations took place in Building 86 at the Portsmouth Naval Shipyard, the structure seen on the upper left of this card. (Author's collection.)

During the Portsmouth Peace Conference, the Russian and Japanese delegations stayed at the Wentworth-by-the-Sea Hotel in New Castle, a short distance from the lighthouse. This image from the summer of 1905 shows military officers leaving a launch and ascending steps onto the presidential yacht. Pres. Theodore Roosevelt was awarded the Nobel Peace Prize in 1906 for his part in the 1905 negotiations. (Library of Congress.)

This c. 1914 photograph shows troops marching outside Fort Constitution. Many changes occurred in the years that followed. A number of buildings were added to Fort Constitution during the World War I era to house an increased number of troops. In 1920, a Coincidence Range Finder Station was built atop a bastion of the old fort to direct the fire of the fort's guns. (Friends of Portsmouth Harbor Lighthouses.)

Henry Cuskley, who was born in Portland, Maine, in 1873, began a 26-year stretch as keeper in 1915. Cuskley began his 44-year career in the US Lighthouse Service as an assistant under Leander White at the Cape Elizabeth "Two Lights" in 1897. At Portsmouth Harbor, Cuskley was involved in community affairs, serving as the chairman of the local school board and on the water commission. He enjoyed giving local children tours of the lighthouse. (Chuck Petlick.)

Henry Cuskley married Mary White, daughter of Leander White. Mary was famous for her Sunday dinners and raspberry custard tarts. One neighbor later claimed that Mary would go into a panic when she got word that the lighthouse inspector was coming. The neighbor said that she "flew around wildly throwing things out the portholes, and I'd run out and catch what I wanted as it flew by. I have a small table today that I caught on the fly." (Chuck Petlick.)

On July 5, 1924, in dense fog, the US Navy destroyer *Brooks* was headed to Portsmouth to refuel when it went aground on a ledge, with the bow only about 15 feet from the lighthouse. There were no injuries, but the forward compartment flooded when a hole was punched in the bow. With the help of two tugboats from the Portsmouth Naval Shipyard, the *Brooks* was refloated a few hours later. (US Navy Bureau of Ships.)

On February 16, 1925, the submarine USS S-48 went aground near the lighthouse. It was able to leave under its own power at high tide. After the grounding, a Navy official wrote, "It is apparent that the lights provided are improper in that there are two fixed red lights on the same side of the channel, namely, Portsmouth Harbor light and Jaffrey Point light." (National Archives.)

The light at Jaffrey Point in Little Harbor, seen here, is about a mile south of Portsmouth Harbor Light. Portsmouth Harbor Lighthouse displayed a fixed white light until 1911, when it was changed to red to avoid confusion with the lights in the nearby towns. After the incident with the S-48, it was changed back to fixed white to avoid being mistaken for the light at Jaffrey Point. In 1934, it was changed to fixed green. It remains a green light today. (Photograph by the author.)

This 1938 photograph of a visitor to the lighthouse shows the fog bell in place but no curtains shielding the Fresnel lens in the lantern room. By this time, a linen cloth was draped over the lens during the day in place of the curtains. The Piscataqua River and Kittery, Maine, are seen in the background. (Author's collection.)

This view from 1946 includes a storage building on the far left that has been demolished in recent years. The entire area seen here is now paved over, and a seawall was added later. The granite 1860s wall of Fort Constitution was never completed, as more powerful and accurate guns aboard ships rendered such walls obsolete. (National Archives.)

New Castle native Arnold White, seen here with his wife, Louise, became keeper in 1942 after serving 20 years as the principal keeper at Whaleback Lighthouse, a mile away at the mouth of the Piscataqua. He was Henry Cuskley's brother-in-law and the son of former keeper Leander White. Arnold White, a civilian keeper for most of his career, joined the Coast Guard when they took over the management of the nation's lighthouses in 1939. He was profiled in a newspaper article during his time at Whaleback. The writer praised White's cooking, saying his dumplings were "an epicurean's dream." Peach pies were said to be another one of his specialties. He explained his general philosophy to the writer: "The government tolerates no excuses. You must anticipate trouble and have spare parts on hand at all times." Arnold White retired in 1946. (Chuck Petlick.)

The next keeper was another veteran of offshore light stations in Maine, Elson LeRoy Small. Small was born in Machiasport, Maine, in 1896, and went to sea at the age of 14. He joined the US Lighthouse Service in 1920 after time as a merchant marine and soon became an assistant keeper at Maine's Lubec Channel Light. Like Arnold White, Small later joined the Coast Guard when they took over the management of the nation's lighthouses. (Friends of Portsmouth Harbor Lighthouses.)

In November 1920, Elson Small married Lubec, Maine, native Constance Scovill. Elson and Connie spent time at four offshore Maine light stations before coming to Portsmouth Harbor: Lubec Channel (1920-1922), Avery Rock (1922-1926), Seguin Island (1926-1930), and St. Croix River (1930-1946). When Connie and Elson moved to the Portsmouth Harbor station in April 1946, it was their first home on the mainland in their married life. It was also the first light station where they had electricity. (Friends of Portsmouth Harbor Lighthouses.)

When Connie and Elson Small moved to the Portsmouth Harbor station in April 1946, it was their first home on the mainland in their married life. One of Connie's duties was to fly weather signal flags from a tower installed by the Weather Bureau of the US Department of Agriculture, signaling mariners of gale or storm warnings. When the flags were damaged and could not be reused, she made quilts from them. (Friends of Portsmouth Harbor Lighthouses.)

Connie Small later said that having electricity for the first time in 1946 was a thrill and that she and Elson went on an "electric binge," buying a washing machine, refrigerator, and other appliances for the keeper's house. At the same time, there was some sadness when she saw that she could turn on the light in the lighthouse by simply pushing a button. The job of lighthouse keeping was suddenly much more impersonal. (Photograph by the author.)

Connie and Elson Small left Portsmouth Harbor Light in 1948. Elson and Connie were hoping for a much longer stay, but the Coast Guard had other plans. It was decided that the lifeboat station on Wood Island, about 4,000 feet away toward the mouth of the river, would be relocated to New Castle in 1948. There would no longer be a resident lighthouse keeper, and the keeper's house became part of the new Coast Guard station. (Friends of Portsmouth Harbor Lighthouses.)

In her book *The Lighthouse Keeper's Wife*, Connie Small described the sad day in May 1948 when she and Elson left the station: "I looked down forty feet to the little white scallops of incoming tide washing over the rocks, caressing each one lovingly. . . I reached for the linen lens cover Elson was holding out to me and wrapped it round the lens like a mother wrapping her baby in its blanket." Pictured are Connie Small with Sally Snowman, keeper of Boston Light, in 2003. (Photograph by the author.)

Seen near the center of this 1947 view from the top of the fort is a coincidence range finder, constructed in 1920. Personnel in this building would help direct fire at enemy vessels with the fort's guns. There was never a shot fired in anger in the fort's history, although 10 people died in an accidental Fourth of July explosion in 1809. (National Archives.)

This 1946 aerial view was taken from a plane out of the Coast Guard air station in Salem, Massachusetts. Most of the buildings have been removed, but the low structure outside the fort wall on the right is used as a research laboratory by the University of New Hampshire. (National Archives.)

Portsmouth Harbor Lighthouse was listed in the National Register of Historic Places in 2009. The National Register application described the architecture of the lighthouse: "The tower is built with six tiers of 12 cast-iron plates each. These are fastened with bolts and nuts. . . . The tower is pierced with three segmental arch windows framed with an exterior decorative cast-iron surround that includes a projecting sill and Italianate hood with triangular pediment. . . . (The lighthouse) embodies and represents distinctive design and engineering characteristics of late nineteenth century cast-iron coastal lighthouses . . . It was constructed during the time when the U.S. Lighthouse Establishment engaged in a concerted effort to replace obsolete or deteriorated lighthouses with cast-iron structures that were better suited to resist deterioration and harsh weather conditions associated with coastal locations. . . . It stands as a monument to New Hampshire's maritime and commercial history, and is widely regarded as a landmark in the Portsmouth Harbor vicinity." (Maine Lighthouse Museum.)

The Sailor's Guardians

Coast Guard crews moved into the former lighthouse keeper's house in 1948. The storm warning tower remained in use, with red lights and flags displayed to indicate storm warnings. The keeper's house remained the center of activity at the Coast Guard station until a new larger building was added to the station in 1967. Today, the former keeper's house serves as offices for the Coast Guard's Marine Safety Detachment. (Friends of Portsmouth Harbor Lighthouses.)

The Coast Guard erected a lookout tower near the shoreline, not far from the lighthouse. The personnel on watch in the tower recorded all boats entering and leaving the harbor and monitored two radios and a telephone switchboard. From 1948 to 1960, when the lighthouse was automated, the man on watch had the added responsibility of turning on the light a half-hour before sunset each day. (Friends of Portsmouth Harbor Lighthouses.)

This c. 1950 image provides a good perspective on the weather signal tower, also known as a coastal warning display tower or storm warning tower. The towers were developed in 1898 on the orders of Pres. William McKinley. Various pennants, flags, and lights were used to indicate small craft advisories, gale warnings, and hurricane warnings. (US Coast Guard.)

This late-1950s view shows the weather signal tower still in place on the left side of the photograph, and the fog bell on the side of the lighthouse. As had been the practice with civilian keepers, the shades in the lantern room were pulled to protect the Fresnel lens. (Friends of Portsmouth Harbor Lighthouses.)

The remains of the 1860s wall of Fort Constitution, the weather signal tower, and the cars of Coast Guard personnel are seen near the former keeper's house in this c. late-1950s view. Coast Guard personnel lived in the keeper's house for some years, beginning in 1948. In 1967, the Coast Guard constructed a large new building on the station to serve as the center of their activities, with a watchtower on its roof. (Bill Johnson.)

In its early years beginning in 1948, the Coast Guard station in New Castle was known as the Portsmouth Harbor Lifeboat Station. The crew posed for this c. late-1950s photograph in front of the old 1808 wall of Fort Constitution, located close to the lighthouse and now a state historic site. The cook, Bill Johnson, was not in this picture because he was preparing the next meal. (Bill Johnson.)

In this c. late-1950s photograph, a young Coast Guardsman at the Portsmouth Harbor Lifeboat Station is hanging his laundry in front of the 1860s wall of Fort Constitution. There was a wringer washing machine in the basement of the former keeper's house for the use of the resident personnel. (Bill Johnson.)

This undated image provides a good look at the stone foundation under the lighthouse, which was built for the 1804 wooden lighthouse tower. For some time, the foundation stones above the high tide mark were whitewashed. The base was severely damaged by storms in 2024. (New Castle Historical Society.)

The old fog bell and striking mechanism were still in operation when the Coast Guard moved in. The person on watch would crank the bell mechanism every two hours in times of fog or poor visibility, and it sounded a single blow every 10 seconds. The "watchstander" would switch the radios and telephones in the lookout tower to an office in the keeper's house when he came down to turn on the light or crank the bell mechanism. The fog bell was deactivated in 1972, and the attached fog signal building was removed. An electronic foghorn was installed on the lantern gallery railing of the lighthouse tower. Today, the horn is operated as needed by mariners in passing vessels using their VHF radios, a system that has been adopted nationwide. The old bell is now displayed outside the main building of Coast Guard Station Portsmouth Harbor. (US Coast Guard.)

There is a mystery regarding when the installation of the fourth-order Fresnel lens that is now in the lighthouse took place, but this photograph offers a clue. It shows a lighthouse technician in 1954 working on the lens in a workshop, indicating that the lens was likely installed around then to replace the lens that had been damaged previously. (*Lighthouse Digest.*)

In this 1957 photograph, a Coast Guardsman can be seen at the top of the watch tower. By this time, with the electrification of the light, the oil house (the small building between the watch tower and the lighthouse) was used for paint storage instead of kerosene storage. (US Coast Guard.)

This c. late-1950s aerial view of Coast Guard Station Portsmouth Harbor and Fort Constitution shows several buildings that were demolished by the mid-1960s. Of the buildings inside the fort, only a small powder magazine remains. The building closest to the fort wall, facing the pier on the left side of the image, is now used as a lab by the University of New Hampshire. (US Coast Guard.)

By the time of this c. late-1950s aerial view, two storage buildings had been added by the Coast Guard next to the keeper's house. The original 1771 lighthouse stood on the rocks at the far right of the photograph. (US Coast Guard.)

This 1960s aerial view was taken after most of the structures inside Fort Constitution had been demolished, but before a new main building had been constructed for the Coast Guard station in 1967. The area on the right with the upside down "12" is where the new main building was constructed. The paved area in the foreground now includes a helipad and a basketball court for the use of the Coast Guard personnel. Coast Guard Station Portsmouth Harbor's personnel protect the state's waterways, conducting more than 70 search-and-rescue operations annually and inspecting maritime cargo. Fort Constitution, located entirely within the Coast Guard station, is a New Hampshire state historic site. In recent years, the fort has been closed to the public, pending repairs. Except for special events, the entire Coast Guard station is currently closed to the general public. (US Coast Guard.)

This view from the early 1970s shows the weather signal tower still in place. The larger of two storage buildings on the left side of the photograph was demolished in the early 2020s. A stairway was later installed on the keeper's house providing access to the lighthouse-facing porch. The 1903 brick oil house, next to the footbridge, was sealed up and in disuse at the time of this photograph. By this time, the shed on the side of the lighthouse that held the hand-cranked striking machinery for the fog bell had been removed, and the bell was sounded with an electrically operated striker. A modern electronic fog signal can be seen mounted outside on the lantern deck of the lighthouse. The new signal began service in 1972. (US Coast Guard.)

The electrically operated fog bell is seen in this c. 1970 view. Much of the ironwork at the top of the tower, along with the entrance door, was painted green by the Coast Guard during this period. This view is from the vicinity of the Coast Guard's new main building on the station, completed in 1967. (Author's collection.)

The blizzard of February 6-7, 1978, was one of the most destructive storms in recorded New England history. Not far to the north, two Coast Guard keepers at Boon Island Lighthouse had to be rescued by helicopter. At Portsmouth Harbor, the wooden footbridge to the lighthouse was partially destroyed by the high seas, as seen in this photograph. It was rebuilt a short time later. (US Coast Guard.)

This view is looking across the Piscataqua River toward Kittery, Maine. Passing by the lighthouse is one of the Coast Guard cutters that was then homeported at Coast Guard Station Portsmouth Harbor. The cutters were eventually relocated to the Portsmouth Naval Shipyard and then in recent years to other parts of the country. (Friends of Portsmouth Harbor Lighthouses.)

This photograph from 1990 shows that the weather signal tower had been removed. The lighthouse was overhauled in 1998 at a cost of more than $73,000. Lead paint was removed from the exterior and interior of the tower, which was then repainted. A rotting wood ceiling in the watch room was replaced with a historically accurate replica as part of the renovation. The base of the tower was refurbished with a new top layer of concrete. (Photograph by the author.)

Portsmouth remains the only deepwater port on the coast between Boston, Massachusetts, and Portland, Maine. The port provides support services for vessels that carry approximately five million tons of cargo in and out of the harbor annually. In this image, a Norwegian tanker passes by in the shipping channel in the center of the Piscataqua River. (Photograph by the author.)

About a mile to the west is the Portsmouth Naval Shipyard in Kittery, Maine. Founded in 1800 during the administration of John Adams, it is the US Navy's oldest continually operating shipyard. Today, most of the shipyard's work concerns the overhaul, repair, and modernization of submarines. Seen here is a submarine leaving the shipyard in 2013. (Photograph by the author.)

The American Lighthouse Foundation was granted a license to care for the Portsmouth Harbor Lighthouse in 2000. Friends of Portsmouth Harbor Lighthouses (FPHL) was founded in the following year as a chapter of the American Lighthouse Foundation. FPHL works for the preservation of both Portsmouth Harbor and Whaleback Lighthouses. For years, the group hosted Sunday afternoon open houses and provided lighthouse tours for thousands of visitors. (Friends of Portsmouth Harbor Lighthouses.)

In recent years, tours of the lighthouse have been by reservation only. Friends of Portsmouth Harbor Lighthouses volunteers provide information on the history of the light stations and their keepers as well as the importance of lighthouses to navigation. Here, volunteer Pete Richard speaks with a tour group in the lantern room. (Bob Trapani Jr.)

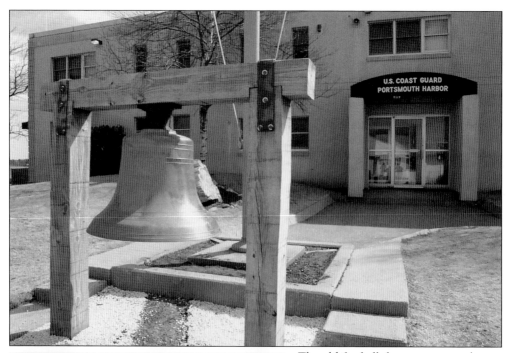

The old fog bell that was mounted next to the lighthouse from 1896 to 1972 is now on display in front of the main building at Coast Guard Station Portsmouth Harbor. The bronze bell was created by the Blake Bell Company, part of W. Blake & Company in Boston. William Blake, the founder, was an apprentice of Paul Revere. W. Blake & Company was in operation from 1820 to 1890. (Photograph by the author.)

The interior of the cast-iron lighthouse tower is lined with brick for added durability, and the brick lining also serves to keep the interior cooler in summer. The 44-step cast-iron stairway, installed when the present tower was built in 1878, is still in place. Portsmouth Harbor Lighthouse is virtually identical, inside and out, to Nauset Light and Chatham Light, erected on Cape Cod at about the same time. (Photograph by the author.)

The automated light at Portsmouth Harbor Lighthouse is serviced periodically by the Aids to Navigation Team South Portland, Maine, otherwise known as ANT South Portland. The work of these teams includes maintenance of lighted and unlighted buoys, lighted and unlighted fixed structures such as day beacons and lights, range lights, and lighthouses. (Bob Trapani Jr.)

On December 23, 2022, a tremendous coastal storm brought offshore seas of more than 25 feet as well as blizzards, high winds, and record-cold temperatures across the majority of the United States and parts of Canada. The storm and the related cold wave killed at least 100 people. The surging waters flooded the Coast Guard station and ripped away more than half of the footbridge to the lighthouse. This was the latest of several times various incarnations of the footbridge have suffered damage in storms over the years. The 2023 tour season was lost due to the damage. Also seen here are some of the unusual rock formations near the lighthouse. The area is considered part of the geographic region known as the Rye Complex, consisting largely of foliated (striated) gneiss and other metamorphic rock. (Dominic Trapani.)

Back-to-back ferocious coast storms on January 10 and 13, 2024, wreaked havoc along the coasts of Maine and New Hampshire. In Maine, more than 20 historic light stations suffered damage. The storm of January 13, which coincided with an usually high king tide, did serious damage to the 1804 stone foundation of the lighthouse. (Dominic Trapani.)

The storm of January 13, 2024, also caused devastating damage to the recently restored 1903 oil house. The oil house, situated on the low-lying rocky beach near the lighthouse, is in harm's way in coastal storms and its long-term survival appears to be threatened, unless it can be somehow protected or moved to safer ground. (Photograph by the author.)

Two

Isles of Shoals (White Island) Lighthouse

The Isles of Shoals are a cluster of nine islands situated several miles off the seacoast of New Hampshire and southern Maine, divided almost evenly between the two states. The low, rocky islands appear smooth, having been scoured by glaciers thousands of years ago. The islands were frequented by European fishermen for years before English captain John Smith explored them in 1614. Smith named the islands Smith's Isles after himself and reported a "silver stream" of cod in the area. It is believed that the name "Isles of Shoals" originated because of the "shoaling," or schooling, of fish around them, and the area remained an important fishing center for centuries. Today, a marine laboratory is based on Appledore, the largest of the islands. A busy conference center has been in operation for a century on Star Island, which is also a destination for local boat companies that bring tourists on day trips. Privately owned Lunging Island, originally known as Londoners after an early cod fishing settlement, has been rumored to be the place where Blackbeard the pirate buried his treasure. Colorful stories of shipwrecks, murder, and ghosts swirl around the islands like a pervasive mist, and White Island figures in some of those stories. White Island Light Station is a vital part of this fabled archipelago.

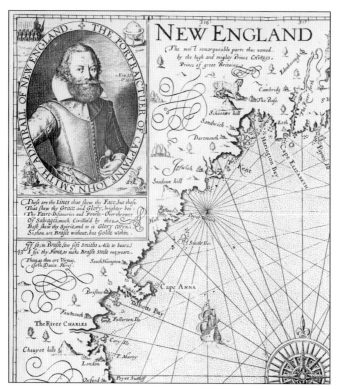

The English explorer John Smith created this map in 1614. Smith had been recruited to survey what was then called North Virginia, and he renamed the region New England. The name "Smith's Isles" did not catch on, as numerous fishermen had been calling the archipelago the Isles of Shoals for years by the time of Smith's visit. (Boston Public Library.)

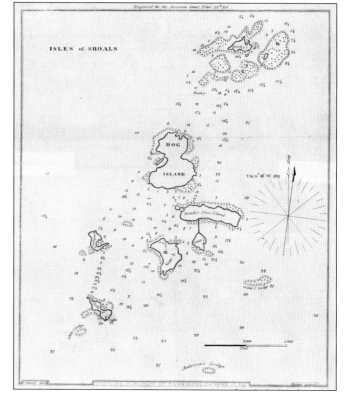

Seen here on an 1837 map, the Isles of Shoals stretch a little more than three miles from north to south. White Island, a barren rock with a steep southern face, is near the lower left corner of this map. What appears to be one island is actually two: White Island to the east and Seavey Island to the west. The two are connected by a bar at low tide. (Library of Congress.)

In May 1820, Congress authorized $5,000 for a lighthouse in the Isles of Shoals. The local customs collector, Timothy Upham, wrote, "After examining carefully all the islands, rocks and shoals, it was the opinion of the gentlemen present that White Island, the southwestern-most of the group . . . was the most suitable, and in fact, the only proper place on which to erect a lighthouse." Carpenter Jonathan Folsom and mason William Palmer constructed a 40-foot tower of "undressed stone, laid in good lime mortar." In the 1840s, the tower was sheathed in wood to prevent leaks. The one-story keeper's house, built of stone, was 28 by 34 feet. Under a separate contract, Folsom built a covered walkway that provided safe passage over the rocks between the dwelling and tower. The lighthouse began service in late 1820 or early 1821 (the exact date is not clear), and the first keeper was Clement Jackson, a local merchant. Jackson had to pay a helper, and his requests for a raise went unheeded. When he resigned in 1824, Jackson was succeeded by a native "shoaler," shipmaster Benjamin Haley. (National Archives.)

The contractor Winslow Lewis installed the original wrought iron lantern and lighting equipment, which consisted of 15 lamps arranged in a triangular framework. The lighthouse was one of the nation's earliest rotating lights with a multicolored characteristic, with alternating red, white, and blue flashes. The blue flash was discontinued in the 1830s because of its poor visibility. This image shows the more efficient second-order Fresnel lens that was installed in 1855. (National Archives.)

Thomas Laighton was appointed keeper in October 1839, after he and his brother bought four of the islands in the Isles of Shoals. Laighton was called "one of the most cranky individuals in all the land or sea" by a local newspaper. He moved to White Island with his wife, Eliza, and their two children, Oscar and Celia. For a time, Laighton served as a Portsmouth selectman from his isolated post. (Author's collection.)

At the age of 16, Laighton's daughter, Celia, married Levi Thaxter, who had been her tutor. The artist William Morris Hunt once told Celia, "You are not afraid, therefore you will be able to do anything." Under the name Celia Thaxter, she later gained widespread fame as a poet and author. Her poetry appeared in the *Atlantic*, *Century*, *Harper's*, and other prominent publications of the day. Most of her poems described aspects of the sea and observations of the Isles of Shoals. One of her most famous poems is *The Sandpiper*, which begins, "Across the lonely beach we flit / One little sandpiper and I / And fast I gather, but by bit / The scattered driftwood, bleached and dry." Celia Thaxter died at the age of 59 and is buried not far from the site of her cottage on Appledore Island. (University of New Hampshire.)

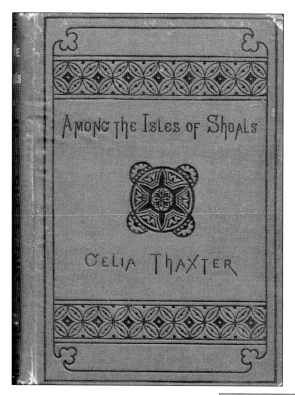

In her 1873 book *Among the Isles of Shoals*, Celia Thaxter described the family's arrival at White Island: "It was at sunset in autumn that we were set ashore on that loneliest, lovely rock, where the lighthouse looked down on us like some tall, black-capped giant, and filled me with awe and wonder . . . Some one began to light the lamps in the tower. Rich red and golden, they swung around in mid-air; everything was strange and fascinating and new." (Author's collection.)

Celia Thaxter also wrote about an evening visit to the water's edge as a young girl: "High above, the lighthouse rays streamed out into the humid dark, and the cottage windows were ruddy from the glow within. I felt so much a part of the Lord's universe, I was no more afraid of the dark than the wave or the winds." (Portsmouth Public Library.)

The Isles of Shoals were assaulted by a terrible storm in December 1839. Celia Thaxter later wrote that she witnessed "the heavily rolling hull of a large vessel driving by to her sure destruction toward the coast." It was the brig *Pocahontas*, wrecked a short time later a few miles to the south. This was the basis of another of Thaxter's best-known poems, *The Wreck of the Pocahontas*. (Watertown Free Public Library.)

William Henry Harrison, a Whig, was elected president in 1840. As a result, Thomas Laighton, who was a Democrat, lost his job as keeper. Joseph Cheever, keeper from 1841 to 1843, hosted the author Richard Henry Dana (pictured) in August 1843. Dana wrote about Cheever in *Vacation Rambles*: "He has taken great pains to perform his duties well, and being an intelligent, temperate man . . . has filled his place better than it has ever been filled." (Author's collection.)

With a change in the political winds, Laighton returned as keeper in 1843. Celia Thaxter's older brother, Oscar Laighton (pictured), was an infant when the family first went to White Island. He described his childhood in his book *Ninety Years at the Isles of Shoals*, writing, "Where our mother dwelt there was happiness also. I am sure no family was ever more united and contented than the Laightons on White Island." Oscar was 16 years old the first time he set foot on the mainland and over 80 the first time he spent a night on the mainland. Although he never became famous as a writer like his sister, Celia, Oscar wrote poetry and also drew sketches—always of fish or sailboats. For the last 30 years of his life, Oscar was a fixture at the conference center on Star Island, where one of his accomplishments was the construction of a new steeple on the island's chapel. He died in 1939, just three months shy of his 100th birthday. (Author's collection.)

The engineer I.W.P. Lewis visited for his report to Congress in 1843. Lewis wrote, "The light is highly important as a point of departure for Portsmouth harbor . . . (T)he red light cannot be seen much more than half the distance of the white, and by a distant observer might be mistaken for the revolving white light of Boston. The whole construction . . . bears the mark of rude workmanship." (Author's collection.)

27th Congress,
3d Session.

Doc. No. 183.

Ho. of Rep.
Treas. Dept.

EXAMINATION—LIGHT-HOUSE ESTABLISHMENT.

LETTER

FROM

THE SECRETARY OF THE TREASURY,

TRANSMITTING

A report from I. W. P. Lewis, civil engineer, upon the condition of the light-houses, beacons, buoys, and navigation, upon the coasts of Maine, New Hampshire, and Massachusetts.

FEBRUARY 25, 1843.
Read, and laid upon the table.

In 1847, the Laightons left White Island for good. A short time later, Thomas Laighton and Levi Thaxter built a large hotel called Appledore House on the largest island in the Shoals. The hotel became a popular summer resort and hosted many high-society guests from Boston and elsewhere, as well as prominent writers and artists of the day. The hotel burned down in 1914. (Library of Congress.)

One of the artists who spent many summers at Appledore House was the American impressionist Childe Hassam. Hassam painted many scenes of White Island and its lighthouse, Appledore, and the other islands in the Isles of Shoals, and he illustrated Celia Thaxter's book *An Island Garden*, a perennial favorite that was first published in 1894. (Library of Congress.)

The author Nathaniel Hawthorne visited White Island in 1852, when L.H.D. Shepard was the keeper. Hawthorne described Shepard in *American Note-Books*: "Since he kept the light, he has lost two wives—the first a young creature whom he used to leave alone upon this desolate rock, and the gloom and terror of the situation were probably the cause of her death. The second wife, experiencing the same kind of treatment, ran away from him." (National Portrait Gallery.)

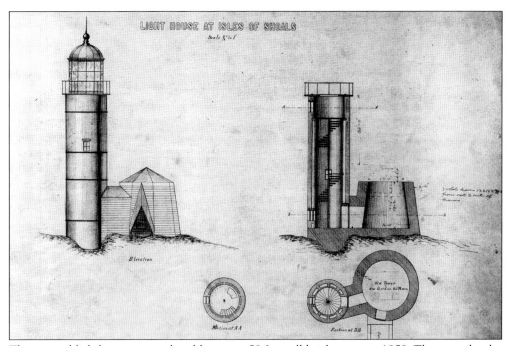

The original lighthouse was replaced by a new 58-foot-tall brick tower in 1859. The second-order Fresnel lens that had been installed in 1855 was moved to the new lighthouse. The lower section of the old lighthouse was left standing next to the new tower, as seen here in the architectural plans. The 1859 lighthouse displays its light from 82 feet above mean high water. (National Archives.)

This photograph was taken soon after the lighthouse was rebuilt in 1859. Three typical "peapod" dories can be seen in the vicinity of the boathouse. This type of dory originated in Maine and was used for lobstering, fishing, and general utility such as tending lighthouses. Peapod dories were sometimes fitted with sails. (US Coast Guard.)

This undated photograph shows the 1859 lighthouse tower, the covered walkway, and an 1892 oil storage building. It's believed that the tower was designed by William Buel Franklin, who at the time was the district lighthouse engineer. Franklin was responsible for a number of influential lighthouse designs, including the twin towers of Thacher Island in Massachusetts. (Penobscot Marine Museum.)

William B. Franklin (1823–1903), designer of the 1859 lighthouse on White Island, graduated at the top of his class at West Point in 1843. In the Civil War, he led a brigade at the Battle of First Manassas and was a commander of a division at the Battle of Fredericksburg. He was taken prisoner by the Confederates in 1864 but managed to escape. (Author's collection.)

There was a legendary rescue in the mid-1800s. John Bragg Downs and a friend were acting as substitute keepers when a severe blizzard hit. They were amazed to discover a lone sailor who had come ashore from a brig wrecked on the rocks. Downs managed to get a line to the remaining crewmen on the vessel. He wedged himself into a crevice and all were able to come ashore. (Author's collection.)

Israel P. Miller was the principal keeper from 1874 to 1876, at a yearly salary of $820. For 1875, Miller counted the following vessels passing White Island during the year: 2 ships, 4 barques, 52 brigs, 56 sloops, 564 steamers, and 20,604 schooners. The most vessels seen passing in one day was 303, on August 27. (Author's collection.)

The nation's first fog bell, at West Quoddy Head in Maine, had just been installed a few months before the establishment of White Island Light Station in 1821. White Island originally had a fog bell that was mounted with striking machinery inside the lighthouse tower, a very unusual arrangement. The 806-pound bell was cast by Joseph W. Revere, the son of Paul Revere. The bell's 10 strokes per minute could not be heard above the thunderous surf, so it was discontinued in 1823. Eventually, the truncated lower portion of the first lighthouse was utilized as a fog bell tower, as seen here. Striking machinery inside the tower had to be wound periodically by the keepers in times of fog. The bell was later replaced by a first-class fog siren, operated with compressed air. (US Lighthouse Society.)

A new Victorian duplex keepers' house—seen here on the left—was built in 1878. David Grogan was the principal keeper from 1880 to 1894. In October 1888, his son Herbert was planning to wed Minnie Rolfe in the lighthouse. Rough weather disrupted the plans, and the wedding took place in South Boston instead. A newspaper account noted the many useful gifts, including a tea set and a pickle jar. This 1888 photograph is credited to H.C. Peabody, Boston.

Along with the construction of the new duplex keepers' house in 1878, the original keepers' house was reconfigured and converted into a storehouse. Five years later, the fuel for the light was changed from lard oil to kerosene. Until the construction of a separate oil house in 1892, the kerosene was probably kept in the storehouse. (National Archives.)

Portsmouth native James Monroe Burke was the principal keeper from 1894 to 1912, after stints at Boon Island and Burnt Island in Maine. He had gone to sea at the age of 14 and eventually skippered fishing vessels before turning to lighthouse keeping. Burke was credited with many rescues during his 18 years at White Island. He once helped 16 women whose pleasure boat had capsized near the island. On another occasion, he saved three persons whose boat was sinking fast. He also rescued four crewmen from the Bangor schooner *Medford* after they had drifted for four days in an open boat. One of his sons, Charles, was a keeper at three different light stations in Maine in the early 1900s. Burke finished his career with seven years at the Cape Neddick "Nubble" Light Station in York, Maine. (Finley family archives and Herb Carpenter.)

James Burke is seen here with his wife, Ida, and their daughter Lucy. After the family left White Island, James was keeper at the Cape Neddick "Nubble" Light, just up the coast from the Isles of Shoals, from 1912 to 1919. Years later, Lucy recalled being carried piggyback by her father, who would wear hip boots for the occasion, across the bar between Nubble Light and the mainland. (Finley family archives and Herb Carpenter.)

This early-1900s photograph shows James Burke and his family at White Island. In January 1911, Burke and his second wife, Addie, were stricken with what a newspaper called "the grippe." Too weak to walk, James resorted to crawling on his hands and knees to tend the light. After six days, a tug captain reached the island in heavy seas and the Burkes were taken to the mainland for medical treatment. (Finley family archives and Herb Carpenter.)

James Burke's wife, Ida, wrote about winter on the island in 1905: "I am feeling much better since the beautiful springtime has come. The mornings are delightful here now, the birds are giving their morning songs, and that seems to put new life into one; while the sun, as it peeps out of the sea so early these fine mornings, seems to bring new strength to go forward to aid life's duties. All through the short days of winter I was kept busy, as we had the assistant to board with us . . . Since that time I have had three men sent by the government to repair what the sea washed to pieces in the heavy storms of winter. The storms were beautiful to watch from the windows, but little [daughter] Lucy was so afraid that she cried with fright, and I kept her in the sitting room, busy cutting out paper dolls, until the storm subsided. Sheets of salt water would strike the windows and sound like the fiercest hailstorm." (Finley family archives and Herb Carpenter.)

Seen at center with members of the Burke family is William Brooks. Brooks was an assistant from 1897 to 1904, after four years at remote Boon Island. He later spent eight years as the principal keeper at the Cape Neddick "Nubble" Light. After years at isolated island light stations, Brooks and his wife liked the Nubble best because of its closeness to the mainland. (Finley family archives and Herb Carpenter.)

Fairfield Moore, a Maine native born in 1871, was an assistant keeper from 1904 to 1909. He went on to have a 24-year career at several lighthouses. He later had three grandchildren born at the Cape Neddick "Nubble" Light Station in York, Maine. His granddaughter Barbara later said that one of her favorite things was going up the stairs and watching her grandfather "light up" for the night. (William O. Thomson.)

Harold Hutchins was an assistant from 1922 to 1924, in the middle of a 25-year career at lighthouses. His wife, Addie, once wrote a poem called *The Lighthouse Sunset*: "I learned a little lesson / As I stood by the lighthouse tall / And gazed at the beautiful sunset / The peacefulness over all./ God's works are all so lovely / Wherever one may be / And I have found contentment / On a lighthouse by the sea." (US Lighthouse Society.)

In 1902, a telephone line reached the island for the first time. A new mechanical striking apparatus for the fog bell was installed in 1905, and then a first-class air siren was installed in 1912. The bell was retained as an emergency backup. An incandescent oil vapor lamp was put in the lantern in 1913. (Author's collection.)

Joseph Upton was principal keeper from around 1915 to 1926. After 23 years at various lighthouses in Maine and New Hampshire, Upton died in 1934 at the Cape Elizabeth (Maine) Light Station. One night, he went to check the light. His wife later found him unconscious after a fall down the stairs. Aged 65, Upton died in a hospital a short time later. (Cape Elizabeth Historical Preservation Society.)

Albert Staples, seen here with unidentified family members, was an assistant keeper from 1926 to 1930. Staples was a distant relative of Fairfield Moore, an earlier keeper. His lightkeeping career spanned from 1914 to 1936 and included stints at four remote island stations in Maine. Staples enjoyed gardening and building his own radios, which he learned by taking a correspondence course from the National Radio Institute. (US Lighthouse Society.)

John Olsen came to White Island as second assistant keeper in 1926. He later spent two years at the Cuckolds Light Station in Maine and then returned as principal keeper at White Island from 1930 to 1935, before finishing his career with nine years at the Cape Elizabeth Light Station in Maine. (US Lighthouse Society.)

For many years, US Lighthouse Service tenders brought supplies to offshore lighthouses. It was reported in June 1932 that the tender *Hibiscus* delivered fresh water to White Island and Whaleback Lighthouse as well as replacing some buoys in the vicinity. For a number of years, all tenders were named for flowers or trees. (US Lighthouse Society.)

This c. 1950s photograph shows heavy surf pounding White Island. In November 1932, the *Portsmouth Herald* reported on a major storm that did much damage on the New Hampshire coast. According to the article, "At high tide waves were breaking over the top of White Island Lighthouse, approximately 150 feet high." The light is, in reality, only 82 feet above the water, and it was most likely only spray that went over the top of the tower. (Author's collection.)

The fog bell seen here served as a backup to a foghorn, which blasted for 190 hours during the month of June 1930. That is 26 percent of the time, which is an unusually high figure. A modern electronic fog signal remains in use today, with a single blast every 30 seconds. The signal is activated by mariners with the use of a VHF radio. (US Coast Guard.)

NOTICE TO MARINERS

Seacoast—NEW HAMPSHIRE

ISLES OF SHOALS
LIGHT STATION

Latitude 42° 58' 02" North; Longitude 77° 37' 25" West

LIGHT TO BE CHANGED

WASHINGTON, December 9, 1930.

About March 2, 1931, the light at Isles of Shoals will be changed to flashing white of 60,000 candle-power, every 15 seconds, thus:

LIGHT 3.7 SECONDS, ECLIPSE 11.3 SECONDS

COMMISSIONER OF LIGHTHOUSES.

A lighthouse's light characteristic refers to the properties that make a particular navigational aid identifiable, such as color and flash patterns. Within a geographic region, all the navigational lights must have distinctive characteristics so they can easily be told apart. On March 2, 1931, the light at White Island went from being an alternating red and white flash to a simple white flash every 15 seconds, rated at 60,000 candlepower. The characteristics of some of the minor lights in Portsmouth Harbor were altered at the same time. The flash sequence at White Island was produced by the Fresnel lens rotating around the light source, which at that time was an incandescent oil vapor lamp that used kerosene as its fuel. The flash pattern at White Island remains the same today. (Author's collection.)

Wilbur "Bill" Brewster, seen here at the Cape Neddick "Nubble" Light Station a few miles up the coast, was first assistant keeper at White Island from 1930 to 1936 and then served as principal keeper into the early 1940s. Brewster was an avid fisherman who spent 26 years in the US Lighthouse Service and Coast Guard, including three years at remote Halfway Rock Light. (Author's collection.)

Like most lighthouses during World War II, White Island Light was extinguished so it would not serve to guide any enemy vessels approaching the coast. Although no surface vessels were spotted, German U-boats were active in the area during the war. When Germany surrendered in 1945, there were at least seven U-boats active in the vicinity, and four surrendered at the Portsmouth Naval Shipyard. (Author's collection.)

On May 23, 1939, the submarine USS *Squalus* was performing test dives nearly four nautical miles south of the Isles of Shoals when a malfunction caused much of the vessel to be flooded, killing 26 men. Using the newly designed McCann rescue chamber, 33 men were successfully rescued. The first responders on the scene were Coast Guard personnel from the station on Appledore Island, just north of White Island. (US Navy.)

Another submarine disaster occurred on June 19, 1941, when the USS O-9 sank during test dives, close to Lunging Island and less than a half mile north of White Island. The sub's entire crew of 33 men was declared lost at sea. Its final resting place remained unknown until a Navy expedition located it in 1997. (US Navy.)

This photograph of a storm sending waves more than halfway up the lighthouse tower at White Island in 1945 calls to mind what keeper Thomas Laighton and his family endured in December 1839. A storm tore wooden sheathing from the lighthouse, and the covered walkway to the tower was destroyed. The barn was also demolished by the storm, but Laighton was able to save the family's cow by moving her into the house. Celia Thaxter described another storm in *Among the Isles of Shoals*: "Before morning the shock of the breakers was like the incessant thundering of heavy guns . . . While the storm was at its height, it was impossible to do anything but watch it through the windows beaten by the blinding spray which burst in flying clouds all over the island, drenching every inch of soil in foaming brine." (Judy Paquette.)

Douglas Larrabee started his lightkeeping career as a civilian at Spring Point Ledge Light in Maine in 1931. In 1939, when the Coast Guard took over management of lighthouses from the old US Lighthouse Service, Larrabee joined the Coast Guard. He was in charge at White Island from 1942 to 1953, then finished his 31-year career as a keeper with nine years at Owls Head in Maine. (Author's collection.)

Pictured here around 1950 are Coast Guard keepers Bill Cannon (left) and John Parks (center), along with Parks's girlfriend, Virginia Hall, next to the Fresnel lens. Parks and Hall were later married. In this era, the Coast Guardsmen's watches on the island consisted of four hours on duty, then eight hours off. (Author's collection.)

This c. 1950 photograph shows the kitchen in the principal keepers' house. A coal stove was used for cooking and heating water. A cistern in the basement held the station's water supply, and the water was pumped to the kitchen sink. Rain was the usual source, but in times of drought, a supply boat delivered water along with whatever else was needed. (Author's collection.)

This 1950 view from the top of the lighthouse shows the two keepers' houses, several outbuildings, fuel storage tanks, and the covered walkway leading to the lighthouse tower. Most of these buildings have been removed over the years. At the time of this image, there was no electricity on the island other than generators. (Author's collection.)

This look inside the second-order Fresnel lens was taken around 1950. The lens was about seven feet tall. This type of lens was the brainchild of Augustin Jean Fresnel in France around 1820, and they came in sizes and strengths from first order down to sixth order. Lenses like the one at White Island had flash panels, or "bullseyes," that produced a flash as the lens rotated around the light source. (Author's collection.)

Near the end of July 1954, an earthquake rattled windows and broke dishes in the New Hampshire Seacoast region. Seaman Philip Hayes, one of the Coast Guard keepers at White Island, said he felt the whole island shake for a few seconds. (Edward Rowe Snow collection, Dolly Bicknell.)

In 1954, a Coast Guard study reported on the status of the 1878 duplex dwelling. The report called the house "surplus to the needs of the station since it is no longer a family station." It was felt that the single dwelling was adequate for the Coast Guard keepers. The duplex had not been used for several years and had deteriorated badly. (US Coast Guard.)

An auction of the house was considered, but the decision was made to demolish it instead. Salvageable items were removed, and Coast Guard personnel quickly razed the building and cleared the site. Seen in the background in this aerial view are Appledore and Star Islands. (US Coast Guard.)

In the late 1950s, the rotation of the Fresnel lens was still regulated by a clockwork-type mechanism with weights suspended from top to bottom inside the lighthouse tower. The machinery was wound at the end of each four-hour watch maintained by the Coast Guard crew. A helipad is seen to the right in this undated aerial view. (US Lighthouse Society.)

Boatswain's Mate Second Class Charles Martin was the Coast Guard's officer in charge from around 1956 to 1958. One year, he decided to try growing pumpkins on the island, but his vine produced just one large pumpkin. Before he could harvest it, a Coast Guard officer visited by helicopter. Martin later sadly recalled, "The blast from the blades knocked the pumpkin from its vine, and it rolled into the ocean." (US Lighthouse Society.)

This 1950s photograph shows a typical "peapod" boat on the ramp in front of the boathouse. Harold Roberts, one of the Coast Guard keepers from 1956 to 1958, later recalled being in the peapod when it capsized after being struck by a huge wave. He was thrown into the water. "The water was bitter cold," he wrote, "The weight of my boots filling with water pulled me down, but the air trapped in my jacket saved me from being pulled down to the bottom. I knew I was in grave danger of drowning. A moment later, the capsized dingy suddenly appeared right next to me. I was able to hold on to the boat to stay afloat." He drifted to the island and was able to crawl ashore. "I believe it was divine intervention that saved my life on that bitter cold winter day on the Isles of Shoals," he wrote. Roberts later became a minister. (Author's collection.)

The great Northeast Blizzard of early February 1978 wreaked havoc all along the New England coast and knocked houses off their foundations in the Boston area, as seen here. At Boon Island Light Station, a few miles up the coast from the Isles of Shoals, the two keepers had to be rescued by helicopter. At White Island, the boathouse was swept away. (National Archives.)

The old second-order Fresnel lens was replaced in the 1970s by a rotating double-head DCB-36 optic. The DCB-36 used a system of plastic Fresnel-type prisms to produce a powerful light; in this case, visible for 21 nautical miles. Developed originally for use at airports, this type of optic was used in many lighthouses but is now very rare. (US Lighthouse Society.)

The DCB-36 optic can be seen in this photograph of the lighthouse tower in the 1980s. Some other changes can also be seen. The original windows in the tower had been replaced with glass block windows, something that was typically done by the Coast Guard in this era. Modern electric fog signals can be seen on the building attached to the lighthouse. The antenna on top of the tower measured wind speed and direction. The Coast Guard keepers at White Island reported weather and sea conditions to Coast Guard Station Portsmouth Harbor. According to Kevin Madison, one of the crew in the 1980s, "Weather was reported by radio to Station Portsmouth Harbor, and when I first got there, it was every three hours. One of us would get up during the night and radio in a weather observation." The requirement was later relaxed so that the weather was only reported during the day. (Kevin Madison.)

This undated photograph shows passengers on a tour boat looking toward White Island. For several decades, companies in the Portsmouth area have offered sightseeing cruises to the Isles of Shoals, with White Island Lighthouse being a prime attraction. The cruises pass Portsmouth Harbor Lighthouse and Whaleback Lighthouse on the way out to the Isles of Shoals. (Mariners' Museum and Park.)

This view shows Star Island in the background. In the 1600s, it was the busiest fishing port on the East Coast. Star is owned and operated as a conference center by the nonprofit Star Island Corporation. The central building was originally the Oceanic Hotel, built in 1873. In its heyday, artists and writers flocked to the hotel. (Mariners' Museum and Park.)

Kevin Murphy was one of the Coast Guard keepers on the island in the mid-1980s. He later said, "We certainly had our share of storms, and there were times we would get stuck out on the island for a month because we couldn't get the dory off the island. Occasionally, we had to be air lifted off the island, which I thought was kind of fun!" (Ed Latta.)

Coast Guardsman Glenn Young was stationed on the island during a memorable storm in March 1984. As 35-foot waves crashed against the lighthouse and keeper's house, the crewmen calmly watched television. The storm did much damage at the station and deposited a 3.5-ton boulder on the helicopter pad. Young took this photograph during another storm years later when he was serving as a caretaker on White Island. (Glenn Young.)

LES OF SHOALS

This early-1980s photograph shows one of the Coast Guard crewmen by the boathouse. The light was fully automated by 1986, with the Coast Guard working with a civilian crew on the process. One of the last men stationed on the island, Kevin Madison, later said, "Although the automation of White Island Light was sad in a way, it was also very interesting." Rick Bennett was the last officer in charge for the Coast Guard. (Ed Latta.)

In 1993, White Island became the first major offshore lighthouse to be converted to solar power by the Coast Guard. Successful completion of this project allowed for subsequent offshore lighthouses to be solarized, greatly reducing the maintenance for the Coast Guard while utilizing an environmentally friendly source of power. (Rear Adm. Daniel R. May, US Coast Guard [Ret.])

The platform on the rear of the solar array was designed so that Coast Guard personnel could access each panel and the electronics control box located in the center of the photograph. The framework was aluminum to prevent corrosion. Each piece was transported to the island and erected by hand. (Rear Adm. Daniel R. May, US Coast Guard [Ret.])

In 1993, ownership of White Island was transferred to the State of New Hampshire and put under the management of the state's Division of Parks and Recreation. Through the rest of the 1990s, the condition of the lighthouse tower deteriorated greatly. Every winter, ice got into cracks and caused many bricks to fall out. (Photograph by the author.)

In the early 2000s, Sue Reynolds, a science teacher at the North Hampton School and a licensed boat operator, launched an effort known as the Lighthouse Kids. The "Kids," made up of seventh-grade students, began a campaign to raise awareness and funds for the restoration of the lighthouse. Sue Reynolds is at the far right in the boat, with her son Pete manning the oars. (Photograph by the author.)

In 2003, the Lighthouse Kids secured a $250,000 federal "Save America's Treasures" grant. Two years later, the Lighthouse Kids presented New Hampshire governor John Lynch with a check for $110,000 that they had raised. The state then authorized the Division of Parks and Recreation to expend additional funds for the restoration of White Island Light Station. (Photograph by the author.)

The lighthouse was repaired in 2005. Damaged bricks were replaced by new bricks, the tower was protected by fresh parging, and window sashes were installed to replace the glass block windows. The roof of the keeper's house was also replaced. The contractor hired for the restoration was Ricci Construction of Portsmouth, while the work on the outside of the tower was done by personnel from J.B. Leslie of Maine. (Photograph by the author.)

The tower's interior iron surfaces, including the entire cast-iron spiral stairway, were repainted by a single worker from F.A. Gray of Portsmouth, a company that has been in business since 1902. The same worker painted the interior ceiling in the lantern room and the exterior domed roof. (Photograph by the author.)

A severe storm in mid-April 2007 destroyed the covered walkway between the keeper's house and the lighthouse tower. The storm left a trail of destruction across the United States, and winds reached 100 miles per hour on top of New Hampshire's Mount Washington with gusts to 156 miles per hour. Eight inches of rain led to floods in New York City. (Photograph by the author.)

This was one of several times over the years that the covered walkway was destroyed in storms, dating back at least to 1839. The powerful storm in April 2007 also swept away the array of solar panels that had been installed in 1993, and the helicopter landing pad was smashed. (Sue Reynolds.)

Pickering Marine of Portsmouth constructed a new marine railway with funds donated by the Lighthouse Kids and the Striped Bass Association. This made it easier to land a boat on White Island, although calm sea conditions are a requirement. (Sue Reynolds.)

In 2011, with the help of federal FEMA funds, a new covered walkway was constructed by Thurston Timber Framers of Concord, New Hampshire. The frames for the walkway were built in a Concord workshop, and Riverside Marine transported the building materials to White Island aboard a barge. A helicopter moved the materials from the barge onto the island. (Photograph by the author.)

Tiny Seavey Island is connected to White Island by a bar at low tide. In 1997, New Hampshire Audubon pioneered a tern restoration project on Seavey. Common terns returned in great numbers, along with endangered roseate and arctic terns. The Nongame and Endangered Wildlife Program at New Hampshire Fish and Game is now responsible for the management of the tern colony. (Photograph by the author.)

White Island (Isles of Shoals) Lighthouse continues as an active aid to navigation, with a solar-powered VLB-44 optic installed by the Coast Guard in 2008. Through a stewardship program launched by Sue Reynolds and the Lighthouse Kids, a series of stewards have stayed in the keeper's house much of the year. (Photograph by the author.)

Three

LAKE SUNAPEE AND A FEW "FAUX" LIGHTHOUSES

Lake Sunapee is in western central New Hampshire, about 10 miles east of the border with Vermont. It is about eight miles long with 70 miles of shoreline. There are 11 islands on the lake with seven beaches on its shores. The state's fifth-largest lake boasts much scenic beauty, but tourism did not arrive until a railroad reached the area in 1872. N.S. Gardner built a bowling alley on one of the islands, and he launched a steamer to carry passengers there. This marked the start of the steamboat era on the lake. The Woodsum brothers launched the *Lady Woodsum* in 1876, capable of carrying 75 passengers. Several grand hotels were soon built along the shores of the lake, along with private estates, and by 1886, five steamships were transporting tourists and summer residents. The Great Depression, along with the prevalence of automobiles, led to the end of the era of steamers on the lake, although the area still attracts many summer visitors.

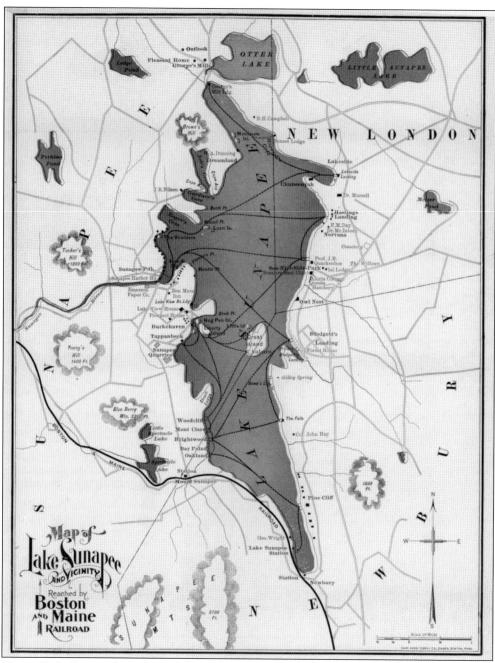

Many of Lake Sunapee's resorts and prominent homes are noted on this 1903 map. The Boulders, on the western shore, was one of the first summer homes on the lake. It was built by A. Perley Fitch, who went from being a druggist in Concord, New Hampshire, to a management position with the Woodsum Steamship Company. Lake Sunapee Station, seen on the map at the lake's southern extremity, was the chief destination of the trains that brought thousands of tourists, many from New York and more distant points. There were few roads and fewer automobiles, so all travel to and from Lake Sunapee was by train and steamship. This 1903 map was published by the Rand Avery Supply Co.

114

Steamships were a prevalent mode of travel on the lake in the late 1800s. In 1891, the 90-foot steamer *Edmund Burke* struck a rock and sank on Lake Sunapee. The Woodsum brothers, Daniel and Frank, were the owners of another steamship. They decided to build wooden lighthouses as navigational aids on the lake. (Author's collection.)

The first lighthouse on Lake Sunapee was erected at a cost of $400 in 1892 on tiny Loon Island, about 1,000 feet off Russell Point on the west side of the lake. In 1896, repairs were being carried out, and the lighthouse caught fire. Firemen put out the fire with lake water using a single bucket. Decades later, in 1960, the lighthouse was struck by lightning and burned down. (Author's collection.)

LIGHT BEARERS: LIFE SAVERS

LIGHT HOUSE, LAKE SUNAPEE, N. H.

New Hampshire Women's Christian Temperance Union.

In 1894, a kerosene lamp was installed in Loon Island Lighthouse, and it used an early type of automation. The unusual lighting system used a lamp was that raised and lowered by a system that used gears and wheels, and it was dimmer during the day. (Author's collection.)

LAKESIDELIGHT LAKESUNAPEE N.H. •70

Herrick Cove Lighthouse, also known as Lakeside Lighthouse, was built a bit later (the exact date is hard to determine) atop a wood and rock crib. It is located on the northeastern part of Lake Sunapee, only about 300 feet offshore. Of the three lighthouses built on the lake, Herrick Cove is the only original one still standing. (Lake Sunapee Protective Association.)

The MV *Mount Sunapee II*, seen here passing by Herrick Cove Lighthouse, has been providing scenic narrated cruises on the lake for decades. The cruises provide views of the lighthouses, landmarks, and scenery of Lake Sunapee, and on a clear day, one can see all the way to Vermont. (Author's collection.)

Burkehaven Lighthouse—only 18 feet tall—was built about the same time as the light at Herrick Cove, a short distance offshore on the west side of the lake. The wooden lighthouse was toppled by ice in 1935, but it was quickly rebuilt. The area known as Burkehaven, a part of the town of Sunapee, is named for the attorney and newspaper editor Edmund Burke. (Author's collection.)

In 1981, the New Hampshire legislature passed a bill that gave the Lake Sunapee Protective Association "the right to repair and maintain" the Herrick Cove and Loon Island Lighthouses. An act in 1983 amended the law to include the newly replaced Burkehaven Lighthouse. (Author's collection.)

Published by Mott L. Bartlett   Loon Island Lighthouse, Lake Sunapee, N. H.

In 1901, the unique lighting system in Loon Island Lighthouse was replaced by an electric light and an underwater cable. The cable worked fine until a fisherman dropped an anchor on it. Some repair work was done to the lighthouse in 1977, and in 1996, the tower was given a new roof and new louvers. (Author's collection.)

In the winter of 2006, under the direction of the Lake Sunapee Protective Association, workers traveled over the ice from the Lake Sunapee Yacht Club and carried out repairs to Loon Island Lighthouse, including the re-siding of the structure with new composite panels that never needed painting. (Lake Sunapee Protective Association.)

By the early 1990s, Burkehaven Lighthouse had developed a tilt due to ice damage in 1992. The tower was dismantled and reconstructed on its new platform by the spring of 1996. Ron Wyman, chair of the Lake Sunapee Protective Association's lighthouse committee, designed a fundraising T-shirt and oversaw the project. (Lake Sunapee Protective Association.)

In 1981, Herrick Cove Lighthouse underwent repairs to rectify a five-degree tilt caused by ice. By 2003, the Herrick Cove crib needed replacement. A helicopter lifted the lighthouse off its base, and the crib was completely rebuilt. In addition, new panels were installed on the lighthouse. Herrick Cove Lighthouse is seen here in the 1990s. (Photograph by the author.)

Loon Island Lighthouse, rebuilt after being destroyed by lightning in 1960, continues to function with a solar-powered light and is an icon of the Sunapee region. Generations of area residents have boated around it and sometimes spent time on the little island. One local woman says that as a girl, she was told that a pair of monkeys named Mike and Ike lived on Loon Island. (Photograph by the author.)

It looks more like a lighthouse than some lighthouses do, but the Weston Observatory is not a lighthouse. The granite tower is located some 33 miles from the seacoast, in Derryfield Park in New Hampshire's largest city, Manchester. It is named for James Adams Weston, who was a civil engineer, banker, and mayor of Manchester for four terms in the 1860s and 1870s. He also served two terms as New Hampshire's governor. As mayor, Weston championed projects that aimed to "beautify Manchester's parks and cemeteries." When he died in 1895, Weston left $5,000 in his will for the construction of the observatory that bears his name. The cornerstone was laid in 1896 during Manchester's 50th anniversary celebration, and it was completed in the following year. The top of the 66-foot tower is 386 feet above the ground. (Author's collection.)

The Weston Observatory was used as a spotting post by air-raid wardens in World War II and later housed police transmitters. It is sometimes open for climbing during special events. On a clear day, it is possible to see Mount Monadnock and Mount Washington from the top of the tower. (Author's collection.)

The small stone tower known as Reeds Lighthouse was built by a Boston news photographer, A.B. Reed. It stands on the western side of Newfound Lake in the town of Bristol, about 15 miles west of Lake Winnipesaukee and more than 70 miles from the coast. It never served as an official lighthouse but is a familiar landmark to area residents. Newfound Lake is the fourth-largest lake in New Hampshire, covering 4,100 acres. (Author's collection.)

Lake Winnipesaukee is the largest lake in New Hampshire, covering about 69 square miles. It is located in the foothills of the White Mountains, about 40 miles from the coast. Spindle Point is in the northwest part of the lake, jutting southward from the town of Meredith. The tower known as the Spindle Point Lighthouse was built in 1892. (Robert Ames.)

The 40-foot stone tower was constructed by Col. Charles Cummings on his estate to serve as an art studio for his two daughters. The tower is sometimes referred to as the Spindle Point Observatory. Today, it is part of a property known as Camp Spindle, with overnight accommodations available to the public. Distant views are possible from scenic cruises aboard the M/V *Mount Washington*. (WeirsBeach.com.)

The faux lighthouse on Potanipo Pond in the town of Brookline, a few miles west of Nashua in southern New Hampshire, is said to have been built by a local resident more than 50 years ago as a small-scale replica of a lighthouse in Maine—which one remains a mystery. It can be seen from a public boat launch. (Photograph by the author.)

The observation tower in Jefferson, New Hampshire, is another example of a tower that resembles a lighthouse but was built for other purposes. Standing right by the side of Route 2 in the White Mountains, it is known as Carter's Tower. James Richard Carter, owner of a paper company, built a vacation home here in the late 1800s with a tennis court and extensive gardens. (Author's collection.)

The stone tower erected on the grounds of the home was often referred to as "Carter's Tower of Foolishness" or "Carter's Folly." It served for a time as a watchtower to look for fires. There were train tracks nearby and sparks from the coal-fired trains sometimes set fires. Reportedly, the Carter family would rush out with brooms to stop the flames before they spread. Carter's Tower is considered one of the earliest fire towers in the nation, predating the founding of the US Forest Service in 1905. (Library of Congress.)

BIBLIOGRAPHY

D'Entremont, Jeremy. "White Island, New Hampshire, and the Lighthouse Kids." Produced by US Lighthouse Society. *Light Hearted*, November 28, 2021. Podcast, 54:49, episode 149. https://news.uslhs.org/2021/11/28/light-hearted-149-white-island-new-hampshire-and-the-lighthouse-kids/

——. *The Light at Fort Point: A History of Portsmouth Harbor Lighthouse, New Castle, New Hampshire, 1771–2021*. Portsmouth, NH: Friends of Portsmouth Harbor Lighthouses, 2021.

Laighton, Oscar. *Ninety Years at the Isles of Shoals*. Boston, MA: The Beacon Press, Inc., 1930.

National Register of Historic Places registration form for Isles of Shoals Light Station. US Department of the Interior, 1987.

National Register of Historic Places registration form for Portsmouth Harbor Light. US Department of the Interior, 2009.

Porter, Jane Molloy. *Friendly Edifices: Piscataqua Lighthouses and Other Aids to Navigation*. Portsmouth, NH: Peter E. Randall Publisher, 2006.

Small, Constance, *The Lighthouse Keeper's Wife*. Orono, ME: University of Maine Press, 1986.

Snow, Edward Rowe. *The Lighthouses of New England*. New York: Dodd, Mead & Company, 1973.

St. John, Helen. *Inalong, Outalong, Downalong: Reminiscences of New Castle, New Hampshire*. Portsmouth, NH: Peter E. Randall Publisher, 1985.

Thaxter, Celia. *Among the Isles of Shoals*. Boston: Houghton, Mifflin and Company, 1875.

——. *Sandpiper: The Life and Letters of Celia Thaxter*. Francestown, NH: Marshall Jones Company, 1963.

www.lighthousefriends.com

www.newenglandlighthouses.net

LIGHTHOUSE ORGANIZATIONS

Friends of Portsmouth Harbor Lighthouses, a chapter of the American Lighthouse Foundation, works to preserve Portsmouth Harbor Lighthouse in New Castle, New Hampshire, and Whaleback Lighthouse in Kittery, Maine. Seasonal tours of Portsmouth Harbor Lighthouse are offered by reservation only. The organization also offers periodic cruises that pass close to the local lighthouses. See www.portsmouthharborlighthouse.org for more information.

The American Lighthouse Foundation, based in Owls Head, Maine, cares for more than a dozen lighthouses in the Northeast. See www.lighthousefoundation.org to learn more.

Readers can learn more about the efforts of the Lighthouse Kids to preserve White Island (Isles of Shoals) Light Station at www.lighthousekids.com.

More information on the lighthouses of Lake Sunapee can be found on the Lake Sunapee Protective Association's website at www.lakesunapee.org

The US Lighthouse Society, based in Hansville, Washington, works to preserve and share the history and legacy of America's lighthouses and their keepers. See www.uslhs.org to learn more.

DISCOVER THOUSANDS OF LOCAL HISTORY BOOKS FEATURING MILLIONS OF VINTAGE IMAGES

Arcadia Publishing, the leading local history publisher in the United States, is committed to making history accessible and meaningful through publishing books that celebrate and preserve the heritage of America's people and places.

Find more books like this at
www.arcadiapublishing.com

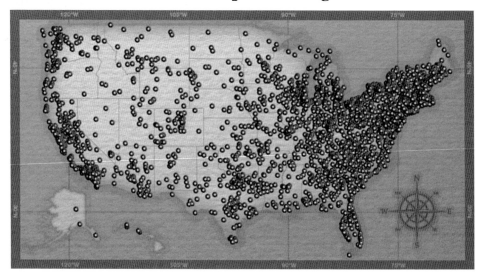

Search for your hometown history, your old stomping grounds, and even your favorite sports team.